A bad attitude is like a flat tyre.
You can't go anywhere
until you change it.

People often say that motivation doesn't last. Well, neither does bathing - that's why we recommend it daily

Jennifer O'Neill

LIFE CHANGING QUOTES

There is only one success - to be able to spend your life in your own way.   **Christopher Morley**

I will not let anyone walk through my mind with their dirty feet.   **Ghandi**

These quotes, like many in this book, have helped to change and shape my life for the better. I trust it will be the same for you.

Wherever possible the original author has been named. However, some quotes have been passed down a long relay of messengers. I would like to thank Jim Rohn for his permission to reproduce some of his great quotes.

I would also like to thank Asa, Reannon and Lyle, my lovely children, who just like these quotes, are a constant inspiration to me. And of course, Rita and Wilf, my fantastic mum and dad, both great role models and a constant support to me.

Barry the Book

About the author

Over the past two decades, Barry Phillips, affectionately known as Barry the Book, has managed 'Knowledge is King' - a family-owned business supplying personal development, motivational and training books and CDs to over a million customers worldwide through mail order and at numerous live events in the UK.

Through his personal journey, meeting and talking to some of the world's top speakers and trainers, he has collected hundred of 'Life Changing Quotes' that have inspired both him and thousands of others to become inspired and to embrace change in their lives.

This second edition of his book has quadrupled in size and is designed to help you unlock the genius within.

Enjoy!

www.knowledgeisking.co.uk

Life Changing Quotes

By
Barry Phillips

Second Edition

Published by
Filament Publishing Ltd
16 Croydon Road, Waddon,
Croydon, Surrey, CR0 4PA
Telephone 020 8688 2598
Email info@filamentpublishing.com
www.filamentpublishing.com

ISBN 978-1-908691- 41-5

Printed by Berforts Information Press
Stevenage and Hastings

Table of Contents

Action

Someday is not a day of the week.

If you never make mistakes, you'll never make anything.

Sir Richard Branson

The most dangerous place to be is in your comfort zone.

If you're not going to make a difference, get out of my way.

Bono

Tell me, I'll forget. Show me, I may remember. But involve me and I'll understand.

Chinese Proverb

Good actions give strength to ourselves and inspire good actions in others

Plato

Life is what we make it, always has been, always will be.

Grandma Moses

Good intentions are no substitute for action

I found every single successful person I've ever spoken to had a turning point. The turning point was when they made a clear, specific unequivocal decision that they were not going to live like this anymore; they were going to achieve success. Some people make that decision at 15 and some make it at 50, and most people never make it at all. **Brian Tracy**

Act quickly, think slowly.

Greek Proverb

Strong reasons make strong actions.

William Shakespeare

I'm not out there sweating for three hours every day just to find out what it feels like to sweat.

Michael Jordan

We are what we repeatedly do.

Aristotle

Everything counts!

You may never know what results come of your action, but if you do nothing there will be no result.

Ghandi

Do it now!

The best way out is always through.

Robert Frost

Bite off more than you can chew, then chew it. Plan more than you can do, then do it.

Many people ignore "small stuff," claiming to have an eye on the bigger picture, never understanding that the bigger picture is composed entirely of small stuff.

Andy Andrews

There is no such thing as trying, either you do it or you don't.

Action

The things that are easy to do, are also easy not to do. That's the difference between success and failure, pennies and fortunes.   **Jim Rohn**

If you want to increase your success rate, double your failure rate.

You'll always miss 100% of the shots you don't take.

Wayne Gretzky

Footprints on the sands of time are not made by sitting down.

Do not wait to strike till the iron is hot; but make it hot by striking.   **William B. Sprague**

It's not what you know, it's what you do. To know and not do is not to know.

Don't wait. The time will never be just right.

Napoleon Hill

What we have to do, we learn by doing.

Even if you're on the right track, you'll get run over if you just sit there. **Will Rogers**

People who want milk shouldn't sit on a stool in the middle of the field in the hope that a cow will back up to them.

Parking meters should remind us that we lose money standing still. **Bert Kruse**

Patience is also a form of action. **Auguste Rodin**

Be not afraid of going slowly, be afraid only of standing still **Chinese proverb**

Stop acting as if life is a rehearsal. Live this day as if it were your last. The past is over and gone. The future is not guaranteed.

Dr Wayne W. Dyer

ACTION

The reward of a thing well done is to have done it.

Ralph Waldo Emerson

Action expresses priorities

Ghandi

Don't be afraid to take a big step if one is indicated. You can't cross a chasm in two small jumps.

David Lloyd George, former Prime Minister

A race horse that can run a mile a few seconds faster is worth twice as much. That little extra proves to be the greatest value.

John D. Hess

Attitude

Ability is what you're capable of doing. Motivation determines what you do. Attitude determines how well you do it.

Lou Holtz

This may shock you, but I believe the single most significant decision I can make on a day-to-day basis is my choice of attitude. It is more important than my past, my education, my bank account, my successes or my failures, fame or pain, what other people think of or say about me, my circumstances or my position. Attitude is that "single string" that keeps me going or cripples my progress. It alone fuels my fire, or assaults my hope. When my attitudes are right, there's no barrier too high, no valley too deep, no dream too extreme, no challenge too great for me.

The choice is up to you, it can either be "Good Morning, God!" or "Good God, morning".

Dr Wayne W. Dyer

A winner's attitude:
it may be difficult,
but it's possible.

A loser's attitude:
it may be possible,
but it's too difficult.

Whenever you're in conflict with someone, there is one factor that can make the difference between damaging your relationship and deepening it. That factor is attitude.

William James

Attitudes are nothing more than habits of thoughts, and habits can be acquired. An action repeated becomes an attitude realised.

Paul Myer

You can complain because roses have thorns, or you can rejoice because thorns have roses.

Zig Ziglar

We can always choose to perceive things differently. You can focus on what's wrong in your life, or you can focus on what's right.

Marianne Williamson

If you don't like something, change it. If you can't change it, change your attitude.

Maya Angelou

What's the difference between an obstacle and an opportunity?   Our attitude towards it!

The greatest revolution of our time is the discovery that human beings, by changing the inner attitudes of their minds, can change the outer aspects of their lives.

William James

If it is to be,
it is up to me!

It is very important to generate a good attitude, a good heart, as much as possible. From this, happiness in both the short term and the long term for both yourself and others will come.

Dalai Lama

Always be anew with the day, just as nature does. It is one of the sensible things that nature does.

George E. Woodberry

Every day, in every way, I'm getting better and better.

Everything can be taken from a man but one thing; the last of the human freedoms - to choose one's attitude in any given circumstances, to choose one's own way.

Viktor Frankl

A man is not finished when he is defeated. He is finished when he quits.

Richard M. Nixon

Never leave it to someone else to decide what you are all about.

The remarkable thing is, we have a choice every day regarding the attitude we will embrace for that day.

Charles R. Swindoll

We choose what attitudes we have right now. And it's a continuing choice.

John Maxwell

There is nothing to
worry about - ever!
Either you have control
or you don't.

If you do, then take control.
If you don't, then dismiss it.
Don't waste energy on worry.

Dr Wayne W. Dyer

No one can make you feel inferior without your consent.

Eleanor Roosevelt

The only difference between ordinary and extraordinary is that little extra.

The winner's edge is not in a gifted birth, a high IQ, or in talent. The winner's edge is all in the attitude, not aptitude. Attitude is the criterion for success. But you can't buy an attitude for a million dollars. Attitudes are not for sale.

Denis Waitley

Attitude is a little thing that makes a big difference.

Winston Churchill

Excellence is not a skill. It's an attitude.

Ralph Marston

Envy is the art of counting other people's blessings rather than your own.

Harold Coffin

If you keep believing
what you've been believing,
then you'll keep achieving
what you've been achieving.

Mark Victor Hansen

Belief

Change your thoughts, change your life.

James Allen

Man often becomes what he believes himself to be. If I keep on saying to myself that I cannot do a certain thing, it is possible that I may end up really becoming incapable of doing it. On the contrary, if I shall have the belief that I can do it, I shall surely acquire the capacity to do it, even if I may not have it at the beginning.

Gandhi

They can because they think they can.

Virgil

**Partial faith is enough to begin.
Once you begin, faith will grow.**

Nurture your mind with great thoughts, for you will never go higher than you think.

Benjamin Disraeli

Fears are like bullies. When you stand up to them, they run away. When you challenge them, they melt and dissipate. When you take bold action, they can't keep up with you.

Believe and act as if it were impossible to fail.

Charles F. Kettering

What the mind of man can conceive and believe, it can achieve.

Napoleon Hill

You have to believe in yourself, that's the secret. Even when I was in the orphanage, when I was roaming the street trying to find enough to eat, even then I thought of myself as the greatest actor in the world.

Charlie Chaplin

To him that believes,
nothing is impossible!

The only thing that stands between a man and what he wants from life is often merely the will to try it and the faith to believe that it is possible.

David Viscott

I was always looking outside myself for strength and confidence, but it comes from within. It is there all the time.

Anna Freud

Why is it so hard for people to believe life should be easy, and so easy for people to believe life should be hard?

Jennifer O'Neill

Who has confidence in himself will gain the confidence of others.

The man who cannot believe in himself cannot believe in anything else. The basis of all integrity and character is whatever faith we have in our own integrity.

Roy L. Smith

Belief

Whether you think you can, or think you can't... you are right.

Henry Ford

We are what we think.
All that we are arises with our thoughts.
With our thoughts, we make our world.

Buddha

Don't back down, just to keep the peace. Standing up for your beliefs builds self-confidence and self-esteem.

Oprah Winfrey

You create your thoughts, your thoughts create your intentions, and your intentions create your reality.

Dr Wayne W. Dyer

You need to believe you'll be successful or you won't be. But you have to believe it before it happens. Most people fail because they can't keep this positive frame of mind until they actually manifest success.

Randy Gage

I found that I could find the energy... that I could find the determination to keep on going. I learned that your mind can amaze your body, if you just keep telling yourself, I can do it... I can do it... I can do it!

Jon Erickson

Faith is to believe what you do not see; the reward of this faith is to see what you believe.

Saint Augustine

What you see is evidence of what you believe. Believe it and you'll see it.

Dr Wayne W. Dyer

You don't get what you don't think about.

Larry James

Only you can think for you.

Belief

When you call yourself a jerk, that is your invisible you judging your invisible self. Remember, what you think about expands.

Dr Wayne W. Dyer

All that a man achieves and all that he fails to achieve is the direct result of his own thoughts.

James Allen

Anything you desire to do, you can do. Anything.

Dr Wayne W. Dyer

Believe as a child believes and the magic will find you.

Teresa Langdon

Believe in your dreams and they may come true. Believe in yourself and they will come true.

Every achiever that I have ever met said, "My life turned around when I began to believe in me."

Dr Robert H. Schuller

Change

> ## There is nothing permanent except change.

If you focus on results, you will never change. If you focus on change, you will get results.

Jack Dixon

As you begin changing your thinking, start immediately to change your behaviour. Begin to act the part of the person you would like to become. Take action on your behaviour. Too many people want to feel, then take action. This never works. **John Maxwell**

You cannot expect to achieve new goals or move beyond your present circumstances unless you change.

Les Brown

Change

If there is anything that we wish to change in the child, we should first examine it and see whether it is not something that could better be changed in ourselves.

Carl Jung

Always remember that the future comes one day at a time.
Dean Acheson

He who rejects change is the architect of decay. The only human institution which rejects progress is the cemetery.
Harold Wilson

It is not the strongest of the species that survive, nor the most intelligent, but the one most responsive to change.
Charles Darwin

If there is no struggle, there is no progress.
Frederick Douglas

The world hates change, yet it is the only thing that has brought progress.

When you are grateful, fear disappears and abundance appears. **Anthony Robbins**

Things do not change; we change.
Henry David Thoreau

When we are no longer able to change a situation, we are challenged to change ourselves.
Viktor Frankl

Time is a dressmaker specialising in alterations.
Faith Baldwin

What you have become is the price you paid to get what you used to want.
Mignon McLaughlin

After you have done a thing the same way for two years, look it over carefully. After five years, look at it with suspicion, And after ten years, throw it away and start all over. It is always your next move.
Napoleon Hill

God, grant me the
serenity to
accept the people
I cannot change,
the courage to change
the one I can,
and the wisdom
to know it's me.

Continuity gives us roots, change gives us branches, letting us stretch and grow and reach new heights.

Pauline R. Kezer

When you blame others, you give up your power to change.

There are three constants in life... change, choice and principles.

Stephen R. Covey

Most of us can read the writing on the wall; we just assume it's addressed to someone else.

Ivern Ball

Change is good - as long as it is managed.

Sir Richard Branson

The only man I know who behaves sensibly is my tailor; he takes my measurements anew each time he sees me.

The rest go on with their old measurements and expect me to fit them.

George Bernard Shaw

Commitment

The moment you commit and quit holding back, all sorts of unforeseen incidents, meetings and material assistance will rise to help you. The simple act of commitment is a powerful magnet for help.

Napoleon Hill

Keep true, never be ashamed of doing right; decide on what you think is right and stick to it.

T. S. Eliot

The prizes of life are at the end of each journey not near the beginning; and it is not given to me to know how many steps are necessary in order to reach my goal.

Failure I may still encounter at the thousandth step, yet success hides behind the next bend in the road. Never will I know how close it lies unless I turn the corner. I will persist until I succeed.

Og Mandino

Right from the beginning, I believed that staying on course was what counted. The sheer process of attrition would wear others down. Them that stuck it out was them that won.

Harrison Ford

Get a good idea and stay with it. Do it, and work at it until it's done right.

Walt Disney

Failure cannot cope
with persistence.

Behold the turtle, he make progress only when he stick his neck out.

James Bryant Conant

Every successful person finds that great success lies just beyond the point where they are convinced the idea is not going to work.

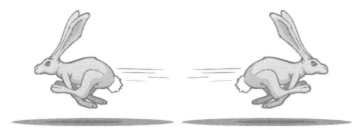

He who chases two rabbits catches none.

Ancient Chinese Wisdom

I never tried quitting, and I never quit trying.

Dolly Parton

Indecision is the seedling of fear.

Napoleon Hill

Winners
never quit
and quitters
never win.

The majority of men meet with failure because of their lack of persistence in creating new plans to take the place of those which fail. **Napoleon Hill**

Nothing in this world can take the place of persistence. Talent will not; nothing is more common than unsuccessful people with talent. Genius will not; unrewarded genius is almost a proverb. Education will not; the world in full of educated derelicts. Persistence and determination alone are omnipotent. The slogan "press on" has solved and always will the problems of the human race.

Calvin Coolidge

Aerodynamically the bumble bee shouldn't be able to fly, but the bumble bee doesn't know it so it goes flying on anyway.

Mary Kay Ash

If better is possible, good is not enough.

Most people never run far enough on their first wind to find out if they've got a second. Give your dreams all you've got and you'll be amazed at the energy that comes out of you.

William James

A certain amount of opposition is a great help to a man. Kites rise against, not with the wind.

John Neal

Choice not chance determine destiny.

Consider the postage stamp: its usefulness consists in the ability to stick to one thing till it gets there.

Josh Billings

Let me tell you the secret that has led me to my goal. My strength lies solely in my tenacity.

Louis Pasteur

The road to success is dotted with many tempting parking spaces.

There are two mistakes one can make along the road to truth - not going all the way, and not starting.

Buddha

Life is not easy for any of us. But what of that? We must have perseverance and above all confidence in ourselves. We must believe that we are gifted for something, and that this thing, at whatever cost, must be attained.

Marie Curie

Measure your commitment by your actions. Your success will follow.

Promises are like crying babies in a theatre, they should be carried out at once.

Norman Vincent Peale

By perseverance the snail reached the ark.

Charles H. Spurgeon

Contribution

Whoever renders service to many puts himself in line for greatness - great wealth, great return, great satisfaction, great reputation, and great joy.

Jim Rohn

Everyone needs to be valued. Everyone has the potential to give something back.

Diana, Princess of Wales

You become successful when you help enough other people to become successful.

We make a living by what we get, but we make a life by what we give.

Winston Churchill

Wealth, like happiness, is never attained when sought after directly. It comes as a by-product of providing a useful service.

Henry Ford

You must be the change you wish to see in the world.

Ghandi

Life is an exciting business, and most exciting when it is lived for others.

Helen Keller

Doing good to others is not a duty. It is a joy, for it increases your own health and happiness.

Zoroaster

You can't help someone up a hill without getting closer to the top yourself.

It is only as we develop others that we permanently succeed.

Harvey S. Firestone

What goes around, comes around.

Dr Wayne W. Dyer

**Give and forget, receive and remember.
Forget injuries, never forget kindness.**

Confucius

No man is so poor as to have nothing worth giving. Give what you have. To someone it may be better than you dare to think.

Henry Wadsworth Longfellow

If you give me rice, I'll eat today. If you teach me to grow rice, I'll eat every day.

Ghandi

If you want one year of prosperity, grow grain.

If you want 10 years of prosperity, grow trees.

If you want 100 years of prosperity, grow people.

Chinese proverb

You don't give just to receive. When asked, "Where did you get that from?" Reannon replied, "I just know it."

Reannon Phillips, age 10

I never wanted to be a businessman. I just wanted to change the world.

Sir Richard Branson

I once gave the refrigerator repairman several of my books and tapes. The repairman asked, "How do you ever expect to make any money when you give away all your stuff?" I replied "When the day comes that you don't have to ask me that question, you'll have the answer."

Dr Wayne W. Dyer

To desire and strive to be of some service to the world, to aim at doing something which shall really increase the happiness and welfare and virtue of mankind - this is a choice which is possible for all of us; and surely it is a good haven to sail for.

Henry van Dyke

The difficulties of life are intended to make us better, not bitter.

Instead of worrying about what people say of you, why not spend time trying to accomplish something they will admire.

Dale Carnegie

The purpose of our life needs to be positive. We weren't born with the purpose of causing trouble, harming others. For our life to be of value, I think we must develop basic good human qualities - warmth, kindness, compassion. Then our life becomes meaningful and more peaceful - happier.

Dalai Lama

Live in such a way, that if someone spoke badly of you, no one would believe it.

Give away that which you most want to receive. If you want more support, give more support. Giving starts the receiving process. And remember that gratitude is the antidote of fear.

Robin Sharma

Here is a test to see if your mission here on Earth is finished: If you're alive, it isn't.

Richard Bach

Courage

If we lived in a world with no fear, then you would never discover the courage you have within.

Jennifer O'Neill

The only way to win

It takes a little courage, and a little self-control.
And some grim determination, if you want to reach the goal.
It takes a deal of striving, and a firm and stern-set chin.
No matter what the battle, if you really want to win.
There's no easy path to glory, there's no road to fame.

Life, however we may view it, is no simple parlour game;
But its prizes call for fighting; For endurance and for grit;
For a ragged disposition and a "don't-know-how-to-quit".

You must take a blow or give one; you must risk and lose.
And expect that in the struggle you will suffer from the bruise. But you must not wince or falter, if you once begin. Be strong and face the battle, that's the only way to win.

Courage is facing your fears. Stupidity is fearing nothing.

Todd Bellemare

Courage does not always roar.
Sometimes courage is the quiet voice
at the end of the day saying,
"I will try again tomorrow."

Being deeply loved by someone gives you strength, while loving someone deeply gives you courage.

Lao Tzu

It takes courage to grow up and become who you really are.

E. E. Cummings

Keep away from people who try to belittle your ambitions. Small people always do that, but the really great make you feel that you, too, can become great.

Mark Twain

Worry is a thin stream of fear trickling through the mind. If encouraged, it cuts a channel into which all other thoughts are drained.

Arthur Somers Roche

You gain strength, courage and confidence by every experience in which you really stop and look at fear in the face. You are able to say to yourself, "I lived through this horror. I can take the next thing that comes along." You must do the thing you think you cannot do.

Eleanor Roosevelt

The things we fear the most have already happened to us.

Deepak Chopra

To overcome a fear, here's all you have to do: realise the fear is there, and do the action you fear anyway.

Peter McWilliams

Courage is being scared to death, but saddling up anyway.

John Wayne

Courage is resistance to fear, mastery of fear - not absence of fear.

Mark Twain

What do we all have in common
with rubber bands ?
We must be stretched
to be effective.

To map out a course of action and follow it to an end requires courage.

Ralph Waldo Emerson

To forgive is to set a prisoner free and discover that the prisoner was you.

Lewis B. Smedes

Fears are like bullies. When you stand up to them, they run away. When you challenge them, they melt and dissipate. When you take bold action, they can't keep up with you.

Pain is temporary, quitting lasts forever.

Lance Armstrong

The day you decide to do it is your lucky day.

Japanese Proverb

He who fears to suffer, suffers from fear.

French Proverb

Excuses are for people
who don't want it bad enough.

The fear of death follows from the fear of life. A man who lives fully is prepared to die at any time.

Mark Twain

The greatest waste in the world is the difference between what we are and what we could become.

Ben Herbster

Let fear be a counsellor and not a jailer.

Anthony Robbins

When you think you can't, revisit a previous triumph.

Jack Canfield

Be who you are and say what you feel, because those who mind don't matter, and those who matter don't mind.

Dr Suess

He who is not everyday conquering some fear has not learned the secret of life.

Ralph Waldo Emerson

The jump is so frightening between where I am and where I want to be... because of all I may become I will close my eyes and leap!

Mary Anne Radmacher

If ever there is tomorrow when we're not together, there is something you must always remember. You are braver than you believe, stronger than you seem, and smarter than you think. But the most important thing is, even if we're apart, I'll always be with you.

Winnie the Pooh

When we least expect it, life sets us a challenge to test our courage and willingness to change; at such a moment, there is no point in pretending that nothing has happened or in saying that we are not ready. The challenge will not wait. Life does not look back. A week is more than enough time for us to decide whether or not to accept our destiny.

Paulo Coelho

Most of the important things in the world have been accomplished by people who have kept on trying when there seemed to be no hope at all.

Dale Carnegie

When the world says, "Give up,"

hope whispers,

"Try it one more time."

Courage leads to heaven; fear to death.

Senaca

F alse

E vidence

A ppearing

R eal

Customer Service

C.A.R.E

Customers Are Really Everything.

If you make a sale, you make a living.

If you make an investment of time and good service in a customer, you make a fortune.

Jim Rohn

The highest of distinctions is service to others.

King George VI

Our customers pay our wages. Let's treat them right and keep them with us.

One good customer well taken care of could be more valuable than £10,000 worth of advertising.

Jim Rohn

Not everyone could be famous, but everybody can be great, because greatness is determined by service.

Martin Luther King Jr.

Earn your customer's trust, and their loyalty will follow.

Sir Richard Branson

Your rewards in life are determined by the problems you solve for others.

No enterprise can exist for itself alone. It ministers to some great need, it performs some great service, not for itself, but for others; or failing therein, it ceases to be profitable and ceases to exist.

Calvin Coolidge

I know of no great man except those who have rendered great services to the human race.

Voltaire

Enthusiasm

Being in a relationship is like getting a new car. In the beginning you are proud of it, you tend to it, and you appreciate and admire it. Later, after the newness wears off you begin to take it for granted, you no longer tend to it and it looses its luster. But remember, your old car is always new to someone else.

Jennifer O'Neill

What I do best is share my enthusiasm.

Bill Gates

Some days there won't be a song in your heart. Sing anyway.

Emory Austin

Be enthusiastic as a leader.
You cannot light a fire with a wet match!

Always remember to
take your Vitamins;

Take your
Vitamin A for Action,

Vitamin B for Belief,

Vitamin C for Confidence,

Vitamin D for Discipline,

Vitamin E for Enthusiasm.

Pablo

The cure for exhaustion is not rest, its enthusiasm.

David Whyte

You will do foolish things, but do them with enthusiasm.

Colette

Ask yourself what makes you come alive, and go do that. Because what the world needs is people who have come alive.

Howard Thurman

Catch on fire with enthusiasm and people will come for miles to watch you burn.

John Wesley

Enthusiasm is the mother of effort, and without it nothing great was ever achieved.

Ralph Waldo Emerson

A man can succeed at almost anything for which he has unlimited enthusiasm.

Charles Schwab

Enthusiasm

The secret of genius is to carry the spirit of childhood into maturity.

**Knowledge is power,
but enthusiasm pulls the switch.**

Ivern Ball

Nothing feels quite as exhilarating as meeting a challenge.

Dr Yosiya Niyo

The best and most beautiful things in the world cannot be seen or even touched. They must be felt with the heart.

Helen Keller

If you can give your son or daughter only one gift, let it be enthusiasm.

Bruce Barton

The real secret of success is enthusiasm.

Walter Chrysler

Some of the world's greatest feats were accomplished by people not smart enough to know they were impossible.

Let us endeavour to live so that when we come to die even the undertaker will be sorry.

Mark Twain

Men who do things without being told draw the most wages.

Edwin H Stuart

Every person is enthusiastic at times. One person has enthusiasm for 30 minutes; another person has it for 30 days, but it is the person who has it for 30 years who makes a success of life.

Edward Butler George

Wherever you go, go with all your heart.

Confucius

Joy is what happens to us when we allow ourselves to recognize how good things really are.

Marianne Williamson

Enthusiasm

It is better to light a candle than to curse the darkness.

Chinese Proverb

A mediocre idea that generates enthusiasm will go further than a great idea that inspires no one.

Mary Kay Ash

If you are not getting as much from life as you want to, then examine the state of your enthusiasm.

Norman Vincent Peale

I studied the lives of great men and women, and I find the men and women who get to the top were those who did the jobs they had in hand, with everything they had of energy and enthusiasm and hard work.

Harry S. Truman

Think excitement, talk excitement, act out excitement, and you are bound to become an exciting person. Life will take on a new zest, deeper interest, and greater meaning.

Norman Vincent Peale

Goals

You become successful the moment you start moving towards a worthwhile goal.

If you greatly desire something, have the guts to stake everything on obtaining it.

Brendan Francis

The only way to achieve true success is to express yourself completely in service to society. First, have a definite, clear practical idea - a goal, an objective. Second, have the necessary means to achieve your ends; wisdom, money, materials and methods. Third, adjust all your means to the end.

Aristotle

Anything inside that immobilizes me, gets in my way, keeps me from my goals, is all mine.

Dr Wayne W. Dyer

In life we get what we order.

"The person who knows how will always have a job. And they'll always be working for the person who knows why"

Gary Ryan Blair

I never wanted to be the next Bruce Lee. I just wanted to be the first Jackie Chan.

Jackie Chan

The more goals you set, the more goals you get.

Mark Victor Hansen

If you have a big enough "why", you'll always discover the "how".

If you don't know where you're going, any road will do.

Dorothy - 'The Wizard of Oz'

The dreams you see most clearly are most likely to come true.

Barney the Dinosaur

The best way to predict the future, is to create it. Start with the end in mind.

The biggest adventure you can ever take is to live the life of your dreams.

Oprah Winfrey

Goals

In failing to plan, you plan to fail.

A goal is not always meant to be reached, it often serves simply as something to aim at.

Bruce Lee

Never worry that your dreams are too big. The Universe and Spirit do not understand limitations, people invented limitations.

Decide what you want, decide what you are willing to exchange for it. Establish your priorities and go to work.

H L. Hunt

The beginning of every great success is desire.

Napoleon Hill

I always wanted to be somebody. Now I see that I should have been more specific.

Lily Tomlin

It's amazing that most people spend more time planning their holiday than their lives. Maybe escape is easier than change.

It's a matter of choice,
make a living,
or design a life.

Be careful what you water your dreams with. Water them with worry and fear and you will produce weeds that choke the life from your dream. Water them with optimism and solutions and you will cultivate success. Always be on the lookout for ways to turn a problem into an opportunity for success. Always be on the lookout for ways to nurture your dream.

Lao Tzu

People are not lazy. They simply have impotent goals - that is, goals that do not inspire them.

Anthony Robbins

Goals

In the absence of clearly defined goals, we become strangely loyal to performing daily trivia until ultimately we become enslaved by it.

Robert Heinlein

Until you commit your goals to paper. you have intentions that are seeds without soil.

When it is obvious that the goals cannot be reached, don't adjust the goals, adjust the action steps.

Confucius

You were born to win, but to be a winner you must plan to win, prepare to win, and expect to win.

Zig Ziglar

The less you think about your future, the more certain it becomes.

Never give up on a dream just because of the length of time it will take to accomplish it. The time will pass anyway.

Jim Rohn

The key to success is to determine your goal, and then act as if it were impossible to fail - and it shall be.

Dorothea Brande

If you deliberately set out to be less than you are capable, you'll be unhappy for the rest of your life.

Abraham Maslow

This one step, choosing a goal and sticking to it, changes everything.

Scott Reed

The major reason for setting a goal is for what it makes of you to accomplish it. What it makes of you will always be of far greater value than what you get.

Jim Rohn

Goals

Goals. There's no telling what you can do when you get inspired by them. There's no telling what you can do when you believe in them. There's no telling what will happen when you act upon them.

We all need lots of powerful long-range goals to help us past the short-term obstacles. The ultimate reason for setting goals is to entice you to become the person it takes to achieve them.

Darren Hardy

If I feel depressed I will sing.

If I feel sad I will laugh.

If I feel ill I will double my labour.

If I feel fear I will plunge ahead.

If I feel inferior I will wear new garments.

If I feel uncertain I will raise my voice.

If I feel poverty I will think of wealth to come.

If I feel incompetent I will think of past success.

If I feel insignificant I will remember my goals.

Today I will be the master of my emotions.

Og Mandino

Habits

Life is like a camera. Just focus on what's important and capture the good times, develop from the negatives and if things don't work out, just take another shot.

Habits are at first cobwebs, then cables.

Spanish Proverb

Don't be afraid to give your best to what seemingly are small jobs. Every time you conquer one, it makes you feel that much stronger. If you do the little things well, the big ones will tend to take care of themselves.

Dale Carnegie

Habits

**Bad habits are like
a comfortable bed,
easy to get into,
but hard to get out of.**

The secret of your future is hidden in your daily routine.

Mike Murdock

Focus 90% of your time on solutions and only 10% of your time on problems.

A J. D'Angelo

Repetition is the mother of skill.

Motivation is what gets you started. Habit is what keeps you going.   **Jim Rohn**

Every person who has become successful has simply formed the habit of doing things that failures dislike doing and will not do.

John Maxwell

You can't build a business on what you're going to do.

It's not the daily increase but daily decrease. Hack away at the unessential.

Bruce Lee

No pain, no gain.

What you don't see with your eyes, don't invent with your mouth.

Jewish Proverb

Don't judge each day by the harvest you reap, but by the seeds that you plant.

Robert Louis Stevenson

Eliminate the word problem, Use opportunity instead.

Every failure is a step to success.

William Whewell

Habits

People decide their habits, their habits decide their future.

What you focus on expands, and when you focus on goodness in your life, you create more of it. Opportunities, relationships, even money flowed my way when I learned to be grateful no matter what happened in my life.

Oprah Winfrey

You'll never go wrong in doing what is right.

The successful always has a number of projects planned, to which he looks forward. Anyone of them could change the course of his life overnight.

Mark Caine

80 percent of your most meaningful results come from 20 percent of your efforts. When you put your focus on that 20 percent, you will make profound, positive change in any area of your life.

The weak can never forgive. Forgiveness is the attribute of the strong.

Ghandi

Fear is a habit; so is self-pity, defeat, anxiety, despair, hopelessness and resignation.

You can eliminate all of these negative habits with two simple resolves:

I can!! and I will!!

Ending Procrastination.

Identify the most important task you have to do today.
Decide to get started with just the first part of the task.
Clear away any distractions, turn everything else off.
Now focus on just starting the task.
Notice the urges to do another task,
notice your mind trying to justify doing something else.
Now just take one small action to get started
and the rest will flow!

Try it now, not later!

We are what

we repeatedly do.

Excellence, then,

is not an act,

but a habit.

Aristotle

Happiness

Happiness is a perfume you cannot pour onto others without getting some on yourself.

Ralph Waldo Emerson

Life naturally evolves in the direction of happiness. We must constantly ask ourselves if what we are doing is going to make us, and those around us, happy. Because happiness is the ultimate goal. It is the goal of all other goals.

Deepak Chopra

Happiness can exist only in acceptance.

George Orwell

The genius of life is to be able to carry the spirit of childhood into adulthood.

The only thing that will make you happy is being happy with who you are, and not who people think you are.

Goldie Hawn

Happiness

If you want to be happy, be.

Leo Tolstoy

You can be as happy as you choose to be.
Happiness is not in having or being, it is in doing.

Lillian Eichler Watson

Being happy doesn't mean that
everything is perfect.
It means that you've decided
to look beyond the
imperfections.

Happiness requires problems...

H.L.Hollingworth

Learn how to be happy with what you have, while you pursue all that you want.

Jim Rohn

Those who laugh... Last

No one can drive us crazy unless we give them the keys.

We take greater pains to persuade others we are happy than in trying to think so ourselves.

Confucius

The happiest people don't have the best of everything. They just make the best of everything.

The basic thing is that everyone wants happiness, no one wants suffering. And happiness mainly comes from our own attitude, rather than from external factors. If your own mental attitude is correct, even if you remain in a hostile atmosphere, you feel happy.

Dalai Lama

Smiles are great investments: the more you collect, the better you feel.

A fool dreams of wealth; a wise man, of happiness.

Turkish Proverb

Happiness

The foolish man seeks happiness in the distance. The wise man grows it under his feet.

James Openheim

It's the ability to take a joke, not make one, that proves you have a sense of humour.

Nobody really cares if you're miserable, so you might as well be happy.

Cynthia Nelms

Happiness is when what you think, what you say, and what you do are in harmony.

Ghandi

It is all perfect, this universe we are in. Slow down and enjoy it all.

Dr Wayne W. Dyer

THE BEST GIFT

It costs nothing.

Takes only one moment to wrap and deliver.

The memory of it can last a lifetime.

It's the only thing we wear that never goes out of style.

One size fits everyone.

A Smile

If someone isn't smiling, give them one of yours!

You would not want to be responsible for someone else's happiness, so please do not hold someone else responsible for yours.

Jennifer O'Neill

Happiness is like a butterfly which, when pursued, is always beyond our grasp, but, if you will sit down quietly, may alight upon you.

Nathaniel Hawthorne

Happiness

We are built to conquer environment, solve problems, achieve goals, and we find no real satisfaction or happiness in life without obstacles to conquer and goals to achieve.

Maxwell Maltz

All blame is a waste of time. No matter how much fault you find with another, and regardless of how much you blame him, it will not change you. The only thing blame does is to keep the focus off you when you are looking for external reasons to explain your unhappiness or frustration. You may succeed in making another feel guilty about something by blaming him, but you won't succeed in changing whatever it is about you that is making you unhappy.

Dr Wayne W. Dyer

If you want others to be happy, practice compassion.
If you want to be happy, practice compassion.

Dalai Lama

Knowledge

Never mistake knowledge for wisdom. One helps you make a living, the other helps you make a life.

Sandra Carey

Mirror, Mirror on the wall, who's the problem after all?

There is a difference between knowledge and wisdom. Knowledge is knowing that a tomato is a fruit, not a vegetable. Wisdom is knowing not to include it in a fruit salad.

Our deepest fear is not that we are inadequate. Our deepest fear is that we are powerful beyond measure. It is our light, not our darkness, that frightens us.

Marianne Williamson

The greatest weakness for many people is that they don't realise their own strengths. What are yours?

Work harder on yourself
than you do on your job,
or career.
If you really want to see
the incredible potential,
you have to step outside
your comfort zone.
It's not what happens to you,
it's how you choose to respond.

The man who makes no mistakes does not usually make anything.

Edward Phelps

You see, in life, lots of people know what to do, but few people actually do what they know. Knowing is not enough! You must take action.

Anthony Robbins

Learning is a treasure that accompanies its owner everywhere. I always tried to turn every disaster into an opportunity.

John D. Rockefeller

Adopt the pace of nature: her secret is patience.

Ralph Waldo Emerson

It's not what we know, but what we use.

Marchant

To know the road ahead, ask those coming back.

Chinese Proverb

Knowledge

Learn from the mistakes of others, there isn't enough time to make them all yourself.
Your mentors in life are important, so choose them wisely.

Robert Kiyosaki

When the student is ready, the teacher will appear.
When the teacher is ready, the student will appear.

Be thankful for what you have; you'll end up having more.
If you concentrate on what you don't have, you will never, ever have enough.

Oprah Winfrey

Gratitude is a quality similar to electricity: it must be produced and discharged and used up in order to exist at all.

William Faulkner

By learning you will teach, by teaching you will learn.

We achieve inner health only through forgiveness –
the forgiveness not only of others but also of ourselves.

Joshua Loth Liebman

Treat the past like a school, learn from it.

Live as if you were to die tomorrow. Learn as if you were to live forever.

Gandhi

The more you read, the more you know. The more you know, the further you go.

The value of an idea lies in the using of it.

Thomas Edison

He who does not use knowledge has no advantage over he who does not have knowledge.

Nourish the mind like you would your body. The mind cannot survive on junk food.

Jim Rohn

A mind once stretched by a new idea, never regains its original dimension.

I have never let my schooling interfere with my education.

Mark Twain

Knowledge

As a rule, he or she who has the most information will have the greatest success in life.

Disraeli

Continuous learning is the key to the 21st century, the information age.

Robert Kiyosaki

Let instruction and knowledge mean more to you than silver or the finest gold. Wisdom is worth much more than precious jewels or anything else you desire.

King Solomon

Knowing others is wisdom, knowing yourself is enlightenment.

Lao Tzu

Imagination is more important than knowledge.

Albert Einstein

The hardest arithmetic to master is that which enables us to count our blessings.

Eric Hoffer

Leadership

The very essence of leadership is that you have a vision. It's got to be a vision you articulate clearly and forcefully on every occasion. You can't blow an uncertain trumpet.

Theodore Hesburgh

Stay committed to your mission and values, even when people doubt you. When people say you'll fail or suggest you're not good enough, stand strong in your own skin and don't let them tear you down.

Michael Jordan

It is wonderful when the people believe in their leader, but it is more wonderful when the leader believes in the people.

It doesn't make much difference how much knowledge or experience you possess, if you are unable to achieve results through people, you are worthless as a leader.

J. Paul Getty

Leadership

Leadership includes both strength and humility.

If you would win a man to your cause, first convince him that you are his sincere friend.

Abraham Lincoln

If you never change your mind, why have one?

Who dares to teach must never cease to learn.

John Cotton Dana

People do not follow programmes, they follow leaders who inspire them.

Leaders must be close enough to relate to others, but far enough ahead to motivate them.

John C. Maxwell

If you share a good idea long enough, it will eventually fall on good people.

**An overdose of praise is like ten lumps
of sugar in coffee; only a very
few people can swallow it.**

Emily Post

Today a reader, tomorrow a leader.

W. Fusselman

One of the greatest gifts leaders can give others is hope.
Never underestimate the power of hope; worlds have
been built on it.

Leadership

The moment you stop learning, you stop leading.

Rick Warren

Leadership is lonely, but it pays very well.

Leaders are made, they are not born. They are made by hard effort.

Vince Lombardi

When you lose, make sure you don't lose the lesson.

You manage things; you lead people.

Grace Murray Hopper

A leader is one who knows the way, goes the way, and shows the way.

John C. Maxwell

Leaders who win the respect of others are the ones who deliver more than they promise, not the ones who promise more than they deliver.

Leaders provide for their people what the people cannot provide for themselves.

John C. Maxwell

Are you a leader?
Turn around and see
who's following you.

Cultivate Patience

Patience is the very heart of love,
Is there a more valuable life skill?
Patience is the best insurance
I know against all kinds
of emotional and
physical problems,
and it is essential for
learning to slow down.

We are not born with it,
however we can all
learn to develop it.
Practice Patience.

Love

Love doesn't make the world go round.
Love is what makes the ride worthwhile.

Franklin P. Jones

Choose your love, love your choice.

Thomas S. Monson

If you wish to be loved, love.

Deep down even the most hardened criminal is starving for the same thing that motivates the innocent baby: Love and acceptance.

Lily Fairchilde

If you have it, you don't need to have anything else, and if you don't have it, it doesn't much matter what else you have.

Sir James M. Barrie

Love is all you need.

John Lennon & Paul McCartney

Love

To fall in love with yourself is the first secret to happiness.

Robert Morley

Where there is love there is life.

Mahatma Gandhi

Whatever the question, love is the answer.

Dr Wayne W. Dyer

You never lose by loving, you always lose by holding back.

Barbara De Angelis

Love deeply and passionately.
You may get hurt
but it's the only way to
live life completely.

Decide that you want it more than you are afraid of it.

Bill Cosby

Friendship isn't a big thing – it's a million little things.

To the world you may be just one person, but to one person you may be the world.

Brandi Snyder

Love is allowing mistakes to be made, and allowing growth to happen as a result of mistakes being made.

Jennifer O'Neill

We've got this gift of love, but love is like a precious plant. You can't just accept it and leave it in the cupboard or just think it's going to get on by itself. You've got to keep watering it. You've got to really look after it and nurture it.

John Lennon

The most beautiful discovery true friends make is that they can grow separately without growing apart.

Elisabeth Foley

Love

Treasure the love you receive above all. It will survive long after your gold and good health have vanished.

Og Mandino

You will find, as you look back upon your life, that the moments that stand out are the moments when you have done things in a spirit of love.

Henry Drummond

The greatest gift that you can give to others is the gift of unconditional love and acceptance.

Brian Tracy

People need love the most when they deserve it the least.
It's easy to love some people.
The true test is to love someone who's hard to love.
Send all your enemies love.

Dr Wayne W. Dyer

You can give without loving, but you cannot love without giving.

Amy Carmichael

You've got to find what you love. And that is as true for your work as it is for your lovers. Your work is going to fill a large part of your life, and the only way to be truly satisfied is to do what you believe is great work. And the only way to do great work is to love what you do. If you haven't found it yet, keep looking. Don't settle. As with all matters of the heart, you'll know when you find it. And, like any great relationship, it just gets better and better as the years roll on. So keep looking until you find it. Don't settle.

Steve Jobs

Your purpose is always about giving, loving, and serving in some capacity.

Dr Wayne W. Dyer

Love

I mourn the loss of thousands of precious lives, but I will not rejoice in the death of one, not even an enemy. Returning hate for hate multiplies hate, adding deeper darkness to a night already devoid of stars. Darkness cannot drive out darkness, only light can do that. Hate cannot drive out hate, only love can do that.

Martin Luther King Jr.

I love you, not only for what you are, but for what I am, when I am with you. I love you not only for what you have made of yourself, but for what you are making of me. I love you for that part of me you bring out.

Roy Croft

If you were going to die soon and had only one phone call you could make, who would you call and what would you say? And why are you waiting?

Stephen Levine

Our Kids

Our kids are our future,
Teach them well!

There are two lasting bequests we can give our children. One is roots. The other is wings.

Hodding Carter Jr.

By giving children lots of affection, you can help fill them with love and acceptance of themselves. Then that's what they will have to give away.

Dr. Wayne W. Dyer

Each day we make deposits in the memory banks of our children.

Charles R .Swindon

When your child's in trouble, open your arms not your mouth.

There is only one pretty child in the world, and every mother has it.

Chinese Proverb

Fifty years from now, it
will not matter what kind
of car you drove,
what kind of house you lived in,
how much you had in
your bank account, or
what your clothes looked like.

But the world may be a little
better place because you were
important in the life of a child.

Our Kids

Kids spell love T-I-M-E

John Crudele

I have found the best way to give advice to your children is to find out what they want and then advise them to do it.

Harry S. Truman

While we may try to teach our children all about life, our children teach us what life is all about.

The doctors told me that I would never walk again.
My mother told me I would. I believed my mother.

Wilma Rudolph, American Athlete

To understand your parents love you must raise children yourself.

Chinese Proverb

Our Kids

The most beautiful sight in the world is a little child going confidently down the road of life after you have shown him the way.

Confucius

Someone once told me that raising a child is a lot like teaching a child to ride a bike. The trick is knowing when to hold on and when to let go.

Joan Marie Saxon

Too often we give children answers to remember rather than problems to solve.

Roger Lewin

Live so that when your children think of fairness and integrity, they think of you.

H. Jackson Brown

**Tell a child they are brave,
and you help them become so.**

Every beetle is a gazelle in the eyes of its mother.

African Proverb

It's not only children who grow. Parents do too. As much as we watch to see what our children do with their lives, they are watching us to see what we do with ours. I can't tell my children to reach for the sun. All I can do is reach for it, myself.

Joyce Maynard

It is easier to build strong children than to repair broken adults.

Frederick Douglass

To be in your children's memories tomorrow, you have to be in their lives today.

When I was a child, my mother said to me, "If you become a soldier, you'll be a general. If you become a monk, you'll end up as the Pope." Instead I became a painter and wound up as Picasso.

Pablo Picasso

Our Kids

Your children need your presence more than your presents.

Jesse Jackson

Children are like wet cement. Whatever falls on them makes an impression.

Haim Ginott

One of the biggest favours that you can do for yourself is to accept your loved ones for who they are, and not be constantly disappointed because they are not who you think they should be.

Jennifer O'Neill

If you keep telling your kids how great they are, they will eventually believe it.

Barry Phillips

If you want children to keep their feet on the ground, put some responsibility on their shoulders.

Abigail Van Buren

Don't handicap your children by making their lives easy.

Robert A. Heinlein

The most important thing that parents can teach their children is how to get along without them.

Frank A. Clark

You can learn many things from children. How much patience you have, for instance.

Franklin P. Adams

If you can give your son or daughters only one gift, let it be enthusiasm.

Bruce Barton

Don't be discouraged if your children reject your advice. Years later they will offer it to their own offspring.

Our Kids

The best thing to spend on your children is your time.

Louise Hart

The most important thing in the world is that you make yourself the greatest, grandest, most wonderful, loving person in the world because this is what you are going to be giving to your children.

Leo Buscagli

As a parent, you have to look at how much time you're spending with your kids. There is nothing you will regret more in your life - nothing - than not being present for your children.

Jamie Lee Curtis

The more you let go the more they grow.

Harry Singha

The best advice from my mother was a reminder to tell my children every day: "Remember you are loved."

Evelyn McCormick

The school will teach children
how to read,
but the environment
of the home must teach
them what to read.

The school can teach
them how to think,
but the home must teach
them what to believe.

Charles A. Wells

People Skills

**It's nice to be important,
but it's more important to be nice.**

You cannot shake hands with a clenched fist.

Ghandi

Beginning today, treat everyone you meet as if he or she were going to be dead by midnight. Extend to them all the care, kindness and understanding you can muster, and do so with no thought of any reward. Your life will never be the same again.

Og Mandino

**If you can't say anything good about
someone, don't say anything at all.**

Men of few words are the best men.

William Shakespeare

When you rearrange the letters of LISTEN you get SILENT.

Brian Koslow

A wise old owl sat on an oak;
The more he saw the less he spoke;
The less he spoke the more he heard;
Why aren't we like that wise old bird ?

Do you wish people to speak well of you?
Then do not speak at all of yourself.

Pascal

Talk is cheap, because supply exceeds demand.
People prefer good listeners to good talkers.

Kind words can be short and easy to speak, but their echoes are truly endless.

Mother Teresa

True friends are like diamonds, precious and rare.
False friends are like fall leaves, found everywhere.

Appreciation can make a day - even change a life.
Your willingness to put it into words is all that is necessary.

Margaret Cousins

People Skill

God gave us two ears and one mouth!

The way to overcome the angry man is with gentleness, the evil man with goodness, the miser with generosity, and the liar with truth.

Indian Proverb

They may forget what you said, but they will never forget how you made them feel.

Carl W. Buechner

One of the greatest gifts you can give to anyone is the gift of attention.

Jim Rohn

Friends are those rare people who ask how you are, and then wait to hear the answer.

I don't like that man. I must get to know him better.

Abraham Lincoln

Treat everyone you meet as if they are the most important person in the world.

You can easily judge the character of a man by how he treats those who can do nothing for him.

Johann Wolfgang Von Goethe

People may doubt what you say, but they will always believe what you do.

The only people with whom you should try to get even are those who have helped you.

John E. Southard

Questions are the key!
If I can say it, that can doubt me
If they say it, it's true.

A man convinced against his will is of the same opinion still.

A B C....
Appreciation
Before Criticism

Communication is the most important life skill.

He who communicates leads.

Seek first to understand, then to be understood.

Don't just listen to what someone is saying, listen to why they are saying it.

He who asks a question is a fool for a minute; he who does not remains a fool forever.

Chinese Proverb

When someone does something good, applaud! You will make two people happy.

Samuel Goldwyn

The surest way to knock a chip off someone's shoulder, is by patting them on the back.

When you are fearful of "important" or "powerful" people, just imagine them using toilet paper.

People Skills

**Smile when picking up the phone.
The caller will hear it in your voice.**

Wise men speak because they have something to say; fools because they have to say something.

Plato

Of all the things you wear, your expression is the most important.

A great people skill is to remember someone's name, and use it often.

The less you talk, the more you will be listened to.

Larry James

Learn how to pay compliments. Start with your family, and you will find it will become easier later in life to compliment others. It's a great asset.

Letitia Baldrige

Personal Growth

The first two rules of personal growth:
1. It will be difficult.
2. It will be worth it.

I will not let anyone walk through my mind with their dirty feet.

Ghandi

Personal growth is the night school and the day school that requires no tuition. It's the greatest university, the best college in this country. You can do more for yourself than anyone else will, or, to put it perfectly plainly, more than anyone else can.

Be not afraid of growing slowly, be afraid only of standing still.

Chinese Proverb

Learning to learn is the biggest learning of all.

Personal Growth

As long as you're green, you're growing.
As soon as you're ripe, you start to rot.

Ray Kroc, founder of McDonald's

What we learn from the past is that we seldom learn from the past.

Use what talents you possess: The woods would be very silent if no birds sang there except those that sang the best.

Henry Van Dyke

The law of the harvest:
Sow a thought, reap an act
Sow an act, reap an habit
Sow a habit, reap a character
Sow a character, reap a destiny

A book is a gift you can open again and again.

Books are like bees carrying the pollen from one person to another.

Gratitude helps you to grow and expand; gratitude brings joy and laughter into your life and into the lives of all those around you.

Eileen Caddy

Good books that are worn out and falling apart usually belong to people who are not.

The book to read is not the one which thinks for you, but the one which makes you think.

James McCosh

In the end, the only people who fail are those who do not try.

I could miss a good meal, but I couldn't miss a good book.

Barry Phillips

Personal Growth

Teachers open the door, but you must enter by yourself.

Chinese Proverb

When the teacher's ready, the student will appear.
When the student's ready, the teacher will appear.

If I cease being better, I cease being good.

Oliver Cromwell

Never regret. If it's good, it's wonderful. If it's bad, it's experience.

Victoria Holt

We can have more than we've got because we can become more than we are.

Jim Rohn

If you do not conquer self, you will be conquered by self.

Napoleon Hill

If you don't run your own life, someone else will.

John Atkinson

Remember, you can never please everyone.

Barry Phillips

We must daily weed the garden of our mind.

Never leave it to someone else to decide what you are all about.

Sometimes adversity is what you need to face in order to become successful.

Zig Ziglar

The only person that you need to be better than is the one you are now.

There is no such thing as a problem without a gift... You seek problems because you need their gifts.

Richard Bach

Opportunity is everywhere.

Personal Growth

When in a hole,
stop digging.

People who reach their potential spend more time asking, "What am I doing well?" rather than, "What am I doing wrong?"

John C. Maxwell

There is a price to pay to grow.
Commitment is the price.

Ed Cole

When you're through growing, you're through.

Dr Wayne W. Dyer

To forgive is to set a prisoner free and discover that the prisoner was you.

Lewis B Smedes

Lots of people want to
ride with you in the limo,
but what you want
is someone who will take
the bus with you
when the limo breaks down.

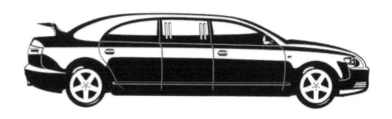

Oprah Winfrey

Every man dies, not every man really lives.

William Ross Wallace

There is only one success - to be able to spend your life in your own way.

Christopher Morley

Success is not the key to happiness. Happiness is the key to success.

Jason Donovan

If I'd observed all the rules I'd never have gotten anywhere.

Marilyn Munroe

**When you are making a success
of something,
It's not work, it's a way of life.
You enjoy yourself because
you are making your
contribution to the world**

Andy Granatelli

Success

The first rule of success, and the one that supersedes all others, is to have energy. It is important to know how to concentrate it, how to husband it, how to focus it on important things instead of frittering it away on trivia.

Michael Korda

**Success isn't about achieving
something in the future,
but about doing something
right now that you love....
So forget about "Success"
and just find "JOY"
"PASSION AND LOVE", in this moment.
This is a Success you can achieve.
Just Do It.**

A successful man is one who can lay a firm foundation with the bricks others have thrown at him.

David Brinkley

Without five years of failing, I couldn't have had one of success. Without a year of building trust with an audience, nobody would've cared about the launch week of my book (except my mom, of course).
And without my wife's constant encouragement, we would've been doomed from the start.
So... the next time you see something that looks like success, remember: it's probably more of a struggle than you think.

Jeff Goins

I never could have done what I have done, without the habits of punctuality, order, and diligence, without the determination to concentrate myself on one subject at a time.

Charles Dickens

Concentrate; put all your eggs in one basket, and watch that basket.

Andrew Carnegie

Success

"The ability to apply your physical and mental energies to one problem incessantly without growing weary."

Reply by Thomas Edison when asked: "What do you think is the first requisite for success in your field, or any other?"

The greatest danger for most of us is not that our aim is too high and we miss it, but that it is too low and we reach it.

Michelangelo

Singleness of purpose is one of the chief essentials for success in life, no matter what may be one's aim.

John D. Rockefeller

The jack-of-all-trades seldom is good at any. Concentrate all your efforts on one definite chief aim.

Napoleon Hill

What do I mean by concentration? I mean focusing totally on the business at hand, and commanding your body to do exactly what you want it to do.

Arnold Palmer

Concentrate all your thoughts on the great desire in your life. This concentration must be continuous, unceasing, every minute, every hour, every day, every week.

Charles E. Popplestone

To do two things at once is to do neither.

Puplilius Syrus

Only those who dare to fail greatly can ever achieve greatly.

Robert Kennedy

You cannot fail, you can only produce results.

Dr Wayne W. Dyer

If at first you don't succeed... follow up

Larry James

Success

Pay now, play later.
Play now, pay later.

John Maxwell

To get to the top in anything you must first get off your bottom.

A person who is successful has simply formed the habit of doing things that unsuccessful people will not do.

Here lies a man who knew how to enlist the services of better men than himself.

Andrew Carnegie's tombstone

Stop focusing on what you do not have, and shift your consciousness to an appreciation for all you are and all that you do have.

Dr Wayne W. Dyer

Is success worth the trouble, the effort, the commitment, the dedication, the perseverance? Yes. Yes, of course it is worth it. The time will pass anyway; why not put it to constructive, productive use? Everybody benefits, nobody loses.

Earl Nightingale

**If you're going to be successful in life,
You're going to have to learn to be
comfortable with being uncomfortable.**

You never achieve success unless you like what you are doing.

Dale Carnegie

You only live once, but if you do it right, once is enough.

Mae West

Today's failure can lead to tomorrow's success.

Sir Richard Branson

I am grateful to all those people who said, "No".

It's because of them that I did it all myself.

Dr Wayne W. Dyer

Time Skill

Time is infinitely more precious than money, and there is nothing common between them. You cannot accumulate time; you cannot borrow time; you can never tell how much time you have left in the Bank of Life. Time is life...

Israel Davidson

Lost

Somewhere between sunrise and sunset - one golden hour encrusted with sixty silver minutes, each studded with sixty diamond seconds. No reward is offered. They are lost and gone forever.

Zig Ziglar

Time is the coin of your life. It is the only coin you have, and only you can determine how it will be spent. Be careful lest you let other people spend it for you.

Carl Sandburg

Time flies... be the pilot.

God gave you a gift of 86,400 seconds today. Have you used one to say, "Thank you"?

William Arthur Ward

Time is our most valuable asset, yet we tend to waste it, kill it and spend it rather than invest it.

Jim Rohn

Don't spend £100's worth of time on a £10 decision.

All great achievements require time.

David J. Schwartz

There is no such thing in anyone's life as an unimportant day.

Alexander Woollcott

Don't serve time, make time serve you.

Willie Sutton

What makes men great is their ability to decide what's important, and then focus their attention on it.

Don't count the days, make the days count.

Muhammad Ali

Procrastination is the thief of time.

Know your priorities so that other peoples' priorities do not become your priorities.

Robin Sharma

Ordinary people think merely of spending time. Great people think of using it.

If you love life, don't waste time, for time is what life is made up of.

Bruce Lee

Wherever you are, be there!

He who every morning plans the transactions of the day and follows out the plan, carries a thread that will guide him through the maze of the most busy life. But where no plan is laid... chaos will soon reign.

Victor Hugo

We gain the advantage in any situation through one medium, time. We gain the advantage by doing things before they need to be done.

You will never find the time for anything. If you want time, you must make it.

Charles Baxton

Nothing is a waste of time if you use the experience wisely.

Auguste Rodin

When you do things you ought to do when you ought to do them, the day will come when you do the things you want to do when you want to do them.

Zig Ziglar

It is never too late to be what you might have been.

George Elliot

I never worry about the future. It comes soon enough.

Albert Einstein

Do one thing every day that scares you.

Eleanor Roosevelt

Write down the most important things you have to do tomorrow. Now, number them in order of their true importance. Then first thing tomorrow morning, start working on item number 1, and stay with it until completed. Then take item number 2 the same way. Then number 3, and so on. Don't worry if you don't complete everything on the schedule. At least you will have completed the most important projects before getting to the less important ones.

Ivy Lee

And in the end, it's not the years in your life that count. It's the life in your years.

Abraham Lincoln

The main reason highly successful people get what they want in life is because they take the time and effort to seriously think what exactly it is they want.

They define their desires in clear & gripping detail..... Another reason is they never settle for anything else. Once they have the goal, they charge ahead regardless of what others think. They never let anyone steal their dreams.

Vision

The greatest tragedy in life is people who have sight, but no vision.

Helen Keller

When there is no vision, the people perish.

Proverb

Reach for the skies, it's closer than you think.

Sir Richard Branson

Ambition is putting a ladder against the sky.

American Proverb

Live out of your imagination instead of out of your memory.

Les Brown

Don't let your past eat your future

I figured that if I said it enough, I would convince the world that I really was the greatest.

Muhammad Ali

Vision

You have to think anyway, so why not think big?

Donald Trump

I saw the angel in the marble and carved until I set him free.

Michelangelo

Great oaks from tiny acorns grow.

There is one quality which one must possess to win, and that is definiteness of purpose, the knowledge of what one wants, and the burning desire to posses it.

Napoleon Hill

Your life will be no better than the plans you make and the action you take. You are the architect and builder of your own life, fortune, and destiny.

We all have possibilities we don't know about. We can do things we don't even dream we can do.

Dale Carnegie

Some people focus on what they are going through; champions focus on what they are going to.

You are never given a wish without also being given the power to make it come true. You may have to work for it, however.

Richard Bach

I expect to spend the rest of my life in the future, so I want to be reasonably sure of what kind of future it is going to be. That is my reason for planning.

Charles Kettering

Always start with the end in mind.

Vision

Far away there in the sunshine are my highest aspirations. I may not reach them, but I can look up and see their beauty, believe in them, and try to follow them.

Louisa May Alcott

If your vision doesn't cost you something, it's a daydream.

John C. Maxwell

Most men die from the neck up by the age of 25 because they stop dreaming.

Ben Franklin

**Without a dream inside you,
there is no dream to come true.**

Gratitude makes sense of our past, brings peace for today, and creates a vision for tomorrow.

Melody Beattie

Never let your memories be greater than your dreams.

Doug Ivester

The best way to turn on your life's vision, is to turn off your television.

The only place where your dream becomes impossible is in your own thinking.

Robert Schuller

The imagination helps us to see reality we have yet to create. A vision is the art of seeing things invisible.

Jonathan Swift

You are the result of all the precious pictures you have painted for yourself... And you can always paint new ones.

Dr Wayne W. Dyer

Live your dreams,
you deserve it.
Enjoy the moment.
Everyone has become so
busy looking ahead and
worrying about their future,
and looking at yesterday
to see what went wrong,
that they are forgetting
to enjoy today.

Wealth

He who is contented is rich

Lao Tzu

Wealth is the ability to fully experience life.

Henry David Thoreau

Early to bed, early to rise,
makes a man healthy, wealthy and wise.

Lack of money is the root of all evil.

George Bernard Shaw

If our schools taught how to become rich, all the teachers would be millionaires.

Rich Dad

I've never been poor, only broke. Being poor is a frame of mind. Being broke is only a temporary situation.

Mike Todd

Wealth

Prosperity depends more on wanting what you have than having what you want.

Albert F. Geoffrey

If you want to be wealthy, study wealth.

A part of all you earn is yours to keep. It should be not less than a tenth no matter how little you earn.

George S. Clason

They say it is better to be poor and happy than rich and miserable, but how about a compromise like moderately rich and just moody?

Diana, Princess of Wales

Those who are of the opinion that money will do everything, may very well be suspected to do everything for money.

George Savile

Anyone who tells you he's not interested in money will lie about other things.

Zig Ziglar

I have not built my business on material wealth . I have built it on relationships. The wealth is a result of the relationships.

Dexter Yager

Any person who contributes to prosperity must prosper in turn.

Earl Nightingale

When I chased after money, I never had enough. When I got my life on purpose and focused on giving of myself and everything that arrived into my life, then I was prosperous.

Dr Wayne W. Dyer

The real measure of your wealth is how much you'd be worth if you lost all your money.

Wealth

Nothing is enough for the man to whom enough is too little.

Epicurus

Ideas are the beginning points of all fortunes.

Napoleon Hill

**To double your net worth,
double your self worth,
Because you will never exceed
the height of your self image.**

Wealth is the product of man's capacity to think.

Ann Rand

The feeling must come first. If you actually feel rich, if you have a deep inner conviction that you will always have all you need, it will be so.

Donald Curtis

Never spend your money before you have it.

Thomas Jefferson

Money is like manure. Just piling it up does no good; you need to spread it around.

A single idea - the sudden flash of a thought - may be worth a million dollars.

Robert Collier

Think and grow rich!

Napoleon Hill

Today, there are three kinds of people: the have's, the have-not's , and the have-not-paid-for-what-they-have's.

Earl Wilson

Despite the cost of living . .
it's still popular.

Wealth

The first step towards discarding a scarcity mentality involves giving thanks for everything that you have.

Dr Wayne W. Dyer

If you must work for money, find a way to work and be happy.

Robert Kiyosaki

Doing what you love is the cornerstone of having abundance in your life.

Dr Wayne W. Dyer

Want little, and you are not poor. You can have a lot of money and possessions, but if you always want more, you are poorer than the guy who has little and wants nothing.

Empty pockets never held anyone back. Only empty heads and empty hearts can do that.

Norman Vincent Peale

Being rich is having money, being wealthy is having time.

Margaret Bonnano

You can make a lot of money
and still think like a peasant.
If you think like a poor person,
no matter how much money
you make, you'll spend it all
and end up poor.

Robert Kiyosaki

I wept because I had no shoes,
until I met a man who had no feet

Ancient Persian Saying

Wealth

Wisdom

Birthdays are good for you. The more you have, the longer you live.

Even death is not to be feared by one who has lived wisely.

Buddha

Reality is merely an illusion, albeit a very persistent one.

Albert Einstein

Our greatest glory is not in never falling, but in getting up every time we do.

Confucius

Letting go is a lot harder than holding on.

Problems are messages.

Shakti Gawain

Would you change your thoughts if you knew they would become reality ?

Blaming is so much easier than taking responsibility, because if you take responsibility... then you might be to blame.

Jennifer O'Neill

We teach people how to treat us.
You either teach people to treat you with
dignity and respect, or you don't.
This means you are partly responsible
for the mistreatment you get at
the hands of someone else.
You shape others' behaviour
when you teach them what they can get
away with and what they cannot.

Great spirits have always encountered violent opposition from mediocre minds.

Albert Einstein

Wisdom

You don't stop dancing because you grow old, you grow old because you stop dancing.

I have always believed that you can bloom and grow wherever you are planted.

Hillary Clinton

Never discuss a problem with someone incapable of solving it.

Feeling gratitude and not expressing it is like wrapping a present and not giving it.

William Arthur Ward

A wise man makes his own decisions; an ignorant man follows public opinion.

Chinese Proverb

Be brave. Take risks. Nothing can substitute experience.

Paulo Coelho

When a deep injury is done us, we never recover until we forgive.

Alan Paton

Adversity introduces a man to himself.

The highest form of wisdom is kindness.

The Talmud

My religion is very simple. My religion is kindness.

Dalai Lama

Honesty is the first chapter in the book of wisdom.

Thomas Jefferson

Control what you can control, accept what you cannot control and learn the difference between the two.

When you find peace within yourself, you become the kind of person who can live at peace with others.

Peace Pilgrim

Wisdom

The key to everything is patience. You get the chicken by hatching the egg, not by smashing it.

Arnold H. Glasgow

There are only two ways to live your life. One is as though nothing is a miracle. The other is as though everything is a miracle.

Albert Einstein

Everything has beauty, but not everyone sees it.

Confucius

Fear an ignorant man more than a lion.

Turkish Proverb

The best things in life aren't things.

The books that help you most are those which make you think the most.

Theodore Parker

Everything is perfect in the universe - even your desire to improve it.

Dr Wayne W. Dyer

"Why not" is a slogan for an interesting life.

Clear your mind of can't.

Dr Samuel Jackson

Try not to take things personally; what people say about you is a reflection of them, not you.

As I grow older, I pay less attention to what people say. I just watch what they do.

Andrew Carnegie

What seems to us as bitter trials are often blessings in disguise.

Oscar Wilde

Wisdom

The difficulties of life are intended to make us better, not bitter.

What the caterpillar calls the end, the rest of the world calls a butterfly.

Lao Tzu

All of the hurdles in your mind that you need to overcome, you've put there.

You cannot be lonely if you like the person you're alone with.

Dr Wayne W. Dyer

What a wonderful life I've had, I only wish I'd realised it sooner.

Colette

There's always something to be thankful for. If you can't pay your bills, you can be thankful you're not one of your creditors.

Wisdom is the reward you get
for a lifetime of listening
when you'd have
preferred to talk.

Work hard and work smart

No rules for success will work if you don't.

I have no idea what motivated me to try again. I felt like giving it a shot. Failure taught me that failure isn't the end unless you give up.

Jim Carey

Ideas don't work unless you do.
Whatever you do today . . .
Do it better tomorrow.

I hated every minute of training, but I said, "Don't quit. Suffer now and live the rest of your life as a champion."

Muhammad Ali

All things are difficult before they are easy.
Short cuts never pay off in the long run.

John Maxwell

Work hard, and you will be a leader. Be lazy, and you will be a slave.

Solomon

Give me six hours to chop down a tree and I will spend the first four sharpening the axe.

Abraham Lincoln

Nothing is particularly hard if you divide it into small jobs.

Henry Ford

Entrepreneur = someone who will work 24 hours a day for themselves to avoid working 1 hour a day for someone else.

It is easier to ride a camel in the direction it is going.

North African proverb

Work hard and work smart

Unless you are willing to drench in your work beyond the capacity of average man, you are just not cut out for positions at the top.

J. C. Penny

There has never been a person in our history who led a life of ease whose name is worth remembering.

Theodore Roosevelt

Pay now, play later.
Play now, pay later.

John Maxwell

Fall seven times, stand up eight.

Japanese Proverb

If at first you don't succeed, fail, fail, fail again.

Most people wish really big yet expect very little, and in life you get what you expect. Expect more of yourself and you will live up to your expectations.

Kurek Ashley

If you don't climb the mountain, you can't see the view.

Things may come to those who wait, but only the things left over by those that hustle.

Abraham Lincoln

It's not the hours that you put in . . .
But what you put in the hours.

Winners take time to relish their work, knowing that scaling the mountain is what makes the view from the top so exhilarating.

Denis Waitley

Work hard and work smart

72% of people who earn in excess of £100,000 a year are early risers.

Some actors pay for someone to pick up their mail, and walk their dog, and pick up their kids from school - but that's your life. So you're paying someone else to live your life so you can work more? I'd rather pay someone to work for me.

Jodie Foster

Sometimes it's easy to work very hard, but on the wrong things - so evaluate regularly.

Get down to business, not busyness!

Do what counts. Focus on what matters.

Larry James

Footprints on the sand of time
are not made by sitting down.

I must do the most productive thing possible at every given moment.

Tom Hopkins

Hard work beats talent when talent doesn't work hard.

I've missed more than
9,000 shots in my career.
I've lost nearly 300 games.
Twenty-six times, I've been trusted
to take the winning shot and missed.
I've failed over and over again in my life.
And that is why I succeed.

Michael Jordan

When I hear somebody sigh, "Life is hard", I am always tempted to ask, "Compared to what?"

Sydney J. Harris

There'll be two dates on your tombstone,
And all your friends will read 'em.
But all that's gonna matter
is that little dash between 'em.

Kevin Welsh

Before you speak, listen.
Before you write, think.
Before you spend, earn.
Before you invest, investigate.
Before you criticise, wait.
Before you pray, forgive.
Before you quit, try.
Before you retire, save.
Before you die, give.

William Arthur Ward

Barry Recommends

The Richest Man In Babylon   George S. Clason

Think and Grow Rich   Napoleon Hill

Rich Dad Poor Dad   Robert T. Kiyosaki

How To Win Friends And Influence People   Dale Carnegie

Listening For Success CD   Steve Shapiro

The Slight Edge   Jeff Olson Book & CD

The Compound Effect 6 CD Set   Darren Hardy

Your Erroneous Zones   Dr Wayne Dyer

You'll See It When You Believe It   Dr Wayne W. Dyer

Excuse Me, Your Life Is Waiting   Lynn Grabhorn

The Top Five Regrets of the Dying   Bronnie Ware

The Day That Turns Your Life Around 6 CD Set   Jim Rohn

Take Charge of Your Life 6 CD Set Jim Rohn

Knowledge is King
25 Hawthorn Close
Wallingford
Oxfordshire
OX10 0SY
United Kingdom
Telephone: +44 (0)1491 201530
Email: sales@knowledgeisking.co.uk